Stations of the Cross
Coloring Book

Color·Prayer·Relax·Repeat Series

mmandiDESIGNS Coloring Books

The Stations of the Cross

A 14-step Catholic devotion that commemorates Jesus Christ's last day on Earth as a man. The 14 devotions, or stations, focus on specific events of His last day, beginning with His condemnation. The stations are commonly used as a mini pilgrimage as the individual moves from station to station. At each station, the individual recalls and meditates on a specific event from Christ's last day. Specific prayers are recited, then the individual moves to the next station until all 14 are complete.

The Stations of the Cross are commonly found in churches as a series of 14 small icons or images. They can also appear in church yards arranged along paths. The stations are most commonly prayed during Lent on Wednesdays and Fridays, and especially on Good Friday, the day of the year upon which the events actually occurred.

Opening Prayer
ACT OF CONTRITION

O my God, my Redeemer, behold me here at Thy feet. From the bottom of my heart I am sorry for all my sins, because by them I have offended Thee, Who art infinitely good. I will die rather than offend thee again.

Your Thoughts • Your Prayers • Your Dreans

First Station: Jesus is condemned to death

We adore Thee, O Christ, and bless Thee.
Because by Thy holy cross Thou hast redeemed the world.
Jesus, you stand all alone before Pilate. Nobody speaks up for you.
Nobody helps defend you. You devoted your entire life to helping
others, listening to the smallest ones, caring for those who were
ignored by others. They don't seem to remember that as they
prepare to put you to death.
As a child, sometimes I feel alone. Sometimes I feel that others
don't stand up for me and defend me when I am afraid.
Sometimes I don't feel like I am treated fairly, especially if I am
scolded or corrected.

As an adult, sometimes I feel abandoned and afraid as well.
Sometimes I too, feel like I am treated unfairly or blamed for
things unfairly. I have a hard time when people criticize me at
home or at work.

Help me be grateful for what you did for me. Help me to accept
criticism and unfairness as you did, and not complain. Help me
pray for those who have hurt me.

My Jesus, often have I signed the death warrant by my sins; save
me by Thy death from that eternal death which I have so often
deserved.

Our Father.... Hail Mary.... Glory Be to the Father....
Jesus Christ Crucified.
Have mercy on Us.
May the souls of the faithful departed, through the mercy of God,
Rest in peace.
Amen.

1st Station: Jesus is condemned to death

Your Thoughts • Your Prayers • Your Dreans

Second Station: Jesus carries His cross

We adore you, O Christ, and we praise you.
Because by your holy cross You have redeemed the world.

Jesus, as you accepted your cross, you knew you would carry it to your death on Calvary. You knew it wouldn't be easy, but you accepted it and carried it just the same.

As a child, sometimes I don't like the problems that come my way. Sometimes I try to get others to take care of them or solve them for me. Sometimes I become upset and crabby when I'm asked to do even the smallest thing to help others.

As an adult I sometimes feel like I'm not appreciated. Sometimes I feel as if I accept more responsibility that I need to. I can feel sorry for myself, even though the crosses others carry are much larger than my own. In my self-pity, I don't reach out to help.

My Jesus, Who by Thine own will didst take on Thee the most heavy cross I made for Thee by my sins, oh, make me feel their heavy weight, and weep for them ever while I live.

Our Father.... Hail Mary.... Glory Be to the Father....

Jesus Christ Crucified.
Have mercy on Us.
May the souls of the faithful departed, through the mercy of God,
Rest in peace.
Amen.

2nd Station: Jesus carries His cross

Your Thoughts • Your Prayers • Your Dreans

Third Station: Jesus falls the first time

We adore you, O Christ, and we praise you.
Because by your holy cross You have redeemed the world.

Jesus, the cross you have been carrying is very heavy. You are becoming weak and almost ready to faint, and you fall down. Nobody seems to want to help you. The soldiers are interested in getting home, so they yell at you and try to get you up and moving again.

As a child, sometimes I start to do something, but then get tired of it. I hurry to get finished and sometimes don't do my work well. Sometimes I don't pay attention to what I should be doing. When things get hard for me, sometimes I give up.

As an adult, I sometimes put things off. I give up too easily, and sometimes don't do my work as well as I know I can.

My Jesus, the heavy burden of my sins is on Thee, and bears Thee down beneath the cross. I loathe them, I detest them; I call on Thee to pardon them; may Thy grace aid me never more to commit them.

Our Father.... Hail Mary.... Glory Be to the Father....

Jesus Christ Crucified.
Have mercy on Us.
May the souls of the faithful departed, through the mercy of God, Rest in peace.
Amen.

Jesus falls the first time

Your Thoughts • Your Prayers • Your Dreans

Fourth Station: Jesus meets his mother

We adore you, O Christ, and we praise you.
Because by your holy cross You have redeemed the world.

Jesus, you feel so alone with all those people yelling and screaming at you. You don't like the words they are saying about you, and you look for a friendly face in the crowd. You see your mother. She can't make the hurting stop, but it helps to see that she is on your side, that she is suffering with you. She does understand and care.

As a child, sometimes I feel like too many things are going on. Sometimes other kids pick on me and call me names. I need to look around me for a friendly face, and for the help I need. I need to share my troubles with those who truly care about me.

As an adult I sometimes feel overwhelmed by many things. Life is so competitive, and I worry so much about my future and those who have some control over it. I need to remember that being an adult does not mean having to solve every problem all by myself. I need to look around me for a friendly face, for the help I need.

Jesus most suffering, Mary Mother most sorrowful, if, by my sins, I caused you pain and anguish in the past, by God's assisting grace it shall be so no more; rather be you my love henceforth till death.

Our Father.... Hail Mary.... Glory be to the Father....

Jesus Christ Crucified.
Have mercy on Us.
May the souls of the faithful departed, through the mercy of God,
Rest in peace.
Amen.

4th Station: Jesus meets his mother

Your Thoughts • Your Prayers • Your Dreans

_____

_____

_____ ___

_____

_____

_____

_____

_____

_____

_____

_____

_____

_____

_____

_____

_____

_____

_____

_____

_____

_____

_____

_____

_____

Fifth Station: Simon of Cyrene helps Jesus to carry his cross

We adore you, O Christ, and we praise you.
Because by your holy cross You have redeemed the world.

Jesus, the soldiers are becoming impatient. This is taking longer than they wanted it to. They are afraid you won't make it to the hill where you will be crucified. As you grow weaker, they grab a man out of the crowd and make him help carry your cross. He was just watching what was happening, but all of a sudden he is helping you carry your cross.

As a child, sometimes I see people who need my help. Sometimes I pretend not to hear when my parents call me. I disappear when I know others could use my help.

As an adult, sometimes I try to do as little as I can and still get by. Others might need my help, but I ignore their needs. Even when I'm asked to help, I sometimes claim to be too busy.

My Jesus, blest, thrice blest was he who aided Thee to bear the cross. Blest too shall I be if I aid Thee to bear the cross, by patiently bowing my neck to the crosses Thou shalt send me during life. My Jesus, give me grace to do so.

Our Father.... Hail Mary.... Glory be to the Father....

Jesus Christ Crucified.
Have mercy on Us.
May the souls of the faithful departed, through the mercy of God,
Rest in peace.
Amen.

5th Station: Simon of Cyrene helps Jesus to carry his cross

Your Thoughts • Your Prayers • Your Dreans

_____

_____

_____

_____

_____

_____

_____

_____

_____

_____

_____

_____

_____

_____

_____

_____

_____

_____

_____

_____

_____

_____

_____

_____

_____

_____

_____

_____

Sixth Station: Veronica wipes the face of Jesus

We adore you, O Christ, and we praise you.
Because by your holy cross You have redeemed the world.

Jesus, suddenly a woman comes out of the crowd. Her name is Veronica. You can see how she cares for you as she takes a cloth and begins to wipe the blood and sweat from your face. She can't do much, but she offers what little help she can.

As a child, sometimes I know someone could use a little help and understanding. They may be picked on or teased by others, or just sad or lonely. Sometimes I feel bad that others don't step in to help, but I don't help either.

As an adult, I notice the needs around me. Sometimes my own family members crave my attention, and I don't even seem to notice. Sometimes a co-worker, friend, or family member could use help or understanding, but I don't reach out to help lest I be criticized, or that they demand more of me than I'd like to give.

My tender Jesus, Who didst deign to print Thy sacred face upon the cloth with which Veronica wiped the sweat from off Thy brow, print in my soul deep, I pray Thee, the lasting memory of Thy bitter pains.

Our Father.... Hail Mary.... Glory be to the Father....

Jesus Christ Crucified.
Have mercy on Us.
May the souls of the faithful departed, through the mercy of God,
Rest in peace.
Amen.

Veronica wipes the face of Jesus

Your Thoughts • Your Prayers • Your Dreans

Seventh Station: Jesus falls the second time

We adore you, O Christ, and we praise you.
Because by your holy cross You have redeemed the world.

This is the second time you have fallen on the road. As the cross grows heavier and heavier it becomes more difficult to get up. But you continue to struggle and try until you're up and walking again. You don't give up.

As a child, sometimes things get me down. Others seem to find things easier to do or to learn. Each time I fail, I find it harder to keep trying.

As an adult, sometimes I think I should know more than I do. I become impatient with myself and find it hard to believe in myself when I fail. It is easy to despair over small things, and sometimes I do.

Help me when things seem difficult for me. Even when it's hard, help me get up and keep trying as you did. Help me do my best without comparing myself with others.

My Jesus, often have I sinned and often, by sin, beaten Thee to the ground beneath the cross. Help me to use the efficacious means of grace that I may never fall again.

Our Father.... Hail Mary.... Glory be to the Father....

Jesus Christ Crucified.
Have Mercy on Us.
May the souls of the faithful departed, through the mercy of God,
Rest in peace.
Amen.

7th Station: Jesus falls the second time

Your Thoughts • Your Prayers • Your Dreans

_____
_____
_____
_____
_____
_____
_____
_____
_____
_____
_____
_____
_____
_____
_____
_____
_____
_____
_____
_____
_____
_____
_____
_____
_____
_____
_____
_____

Eighth Station: Jesus meets the women of Jerusalem

We adore you, O Christ, and we praise you.
Because by your holy cross You have redeemed the world.

Jesus, as you carry your cross you see a group of women along the road. As you pass by you see they are sad. You stop to spend a moment with them, to offer them some encouragement. Although you are have been abandoned by your friends and are in pain, you stop and try to help them.

As a child, sometimes I think a lot about myself. I think about what I want and would like people to spend their lives pleasing me.

As an adult, sometimes I act like a child. I become so absorbed in myself and what I'd like that I forget about the needs of others. I take them for granted, and often ignore their needs.

Help me think more about others. Help me remembers that others have problems, too. Help me respond to them even when I'm busy or preoccupied with my own problems.

My Jesus, Who didst comfort the pious women of Jerusalem who wept to see Thee bruised and torn, comfort my soul with Thy tender pity, for in Thy pity lies my trust. May my heart ever answer Thine.

Our Father.... Hail Mary.... Glory be to the Father....

Jesus Christ Crucified.
Have Mercy on Us.
May the souls of the faithful departed, through the mercy of God, Rest in peace.
Amen.

8th Station: Jesus meets the women of Jerusalem

Your Thoughts • Your Prayers • Your Dreans

Ninth Station: Jesus falls a third time

We adore you, O Christ, and we praise you.
Because by your holy cross You have redeemed the world.

Jesus, your journey has been long. You fall again, beneath your cross. You know your journey is coming to an end. You struggle and struggle. You get up and keep going.

As a child, sometimes I fail time and time again. I find it hard to get along with my sisters and brothers, sometimes I'm not honest, sometimes I'm lazy. I'm tempted to stop trying. It's just too hard sometimes.

As an adult, I often feel I should have conquered my weaknesses by now. I become discouraged when I'm confronted by the same problems over and over again. Sometimes I get weary. When I have health problems, I can become discouraged and depressed.

Help me think of the cross you carried. Help me continue to hope that I can make the changes in my life I need to. You didn't give up. I can have the strength to get up again as well.

My Jesus, by all the bitter woes Thou didst endure when for the third time the heavy cross bowed Thee to the earth, never, I beseech Thee, let me fall again into sin. Ah, my Jesus, rather let me die than ever offend Thee again.

Our Father.... Hail Mary.... Glory be to the Father....

Jesus Christ Crucified.
Have mercy on Us.
May the souls of the faithful departed, through the mercy of God, Rest in Peace.
Amen.

9th Station: Jesus falls a third time

Your Thoughts • Your Prayers • Your Dreans

_____
_____
_____
_____
_____
_____
_____
_____
_____
_____
_____
_____
_____
_____
_____
_____
_____
_____
_____
_____
_____
_____
_____
_____
_____

Tenth Station: Jesus clothes are taken away

We adore you, O Christ, and we praise you.
Because by your holy cross You have redeemed the world.

The soldiers notice you have something of value. They remove your cloak and throw dice for it. Your wounds are torn open once again. Some of the people in the crowd make fun of you. They tease you and challenge you to perform a miracle for them to see. They're not aware that you'll perform the greatest miracle of all!

As a child, sometimes I'm tempted to repeat stories I know are unclean and disrespectful. I sometimes try to act grown up by using crude and bad words.

As an adult, sometimes I repeat stories that are disrespectful of others. I can entertain thoughts that are not clean. Sometimes I give the young people around me a bad example to follow.

Help me to keep myself pure and clean. Help me say things that build up the people around me. Help me overcome worldly desires that I may become more like Jesus. Help me set a good example for others to follow.

My Jesus, stripped of Thy garments and drenched with gall, strip me of love for things of earth, and make me loathe all that savors of the world and sin.

Our Father.... Hail Mary.... Glory be to the Father....

Jesus Christ Crucified.
Have mercy on Us.
May the souls of the faithful departed, through the mercy of God,
Rest in peace.
Amen.

10th Station: Jesus clothes are taken away

Your Thoughts • Your Prayers • Your Dreans

Eleventh Station: Jesus is nailed to the cross

We adore you, O Christ, and we praise you.
Because by your holy cross You have redeemed the world.

You are stretched out on the cross you have carried so far. The soldiers take big nails and drive them into your hands and feet. You feel abandoned by the people you loved so much. People seem to have gone mad. You have done nothing but good, yet they drive nails through your hands and feet.

As a child, sometimes I hurt others. Sometimes I join with friends and decide not to like another. We gang up against another and cause them hurt and pain. Sometimes I say or do hurtful things to my brothers and sisters. I can wonder what they'd think about themselves if they believed everything I told them about themselves.

As and adult, sometimes I discriminate against others. Even without thinking, I judge others because of their color, intelligence, income level or name. I forget that I am to live as a brother or sister to all people. Sometimes I use harsh words when I speak to my children and family members. I can find it easy to look for something that isn't very important and make it very important.

Help me look again at the people around me. Help me see the hurt and pain I have caused in others. Be with me to help me make amends for the harm I have done.

My Jesus, by Thine agony when the cruel nails pierced Thy tender hands and feet and fixed them to the cross, make me crucify my flesh by Christian penance.

Our Father.... Hail Mary.... Glory be to the Father....

Jesus Christ Crucified.
Have mercy on Us.
May the souls of the faithful departed, through the mercy of God,
Rest in peace.
Amen.

11th Station: Jesus is nailed to the cross

Your Thoughts • Your Prayers • Your Dreans

Twelfth Station: Jesus dies on the cross

We adore you, O Christ, and we praise you.
Because by your holy cross You have redeemed the world.

As Jesus hung on the cross, he forgave the soldiers who had crucified him, and prayed for his mother and friends. Jesus wanted all of us to be able to live forever with God, so he gave all he had for us.

Jesus, let me take a few moments now to consider your love for me. Help me thank you for your willingness to go to your death for me. Help me express my love for you!

My Jesus, three hours didst Thou hang in agony, and then die for me; let me die before I sin, and if I live, live for Thy love and faithful service.

Our Father.... Hail Mary.... Glory be to the Father....

Jesus Christ Crucified.
Have mercy on Us.
May the souls of the faithful departed, through the mercy of God, Rest in peace.
Amen.

12th Station: Jesus dies on the cross

Your Thoughts • Your Prayers • Your Dreans

_____
_____
_____
_____
_____
_____
_____
_____
_____
_____
_____
_____
_____
_____
_____
_____
_____
_____
_____
_____
_____
_____
_____
_____
_____
_____
_____
_____

Thirteenth Station: The body of Jesus is taken down from the cross

We adore you, O Christ, and we praise you.
Because by your holy cross You have redeemed the world.

Jesus, how brutally you were put to death. How gently your are taken from the cross. Your suffering and pain are ended, and you are put in the lap of your mother. The dirt and blood are wiped away. You are treated with love.

As a child, sometimes I treat others better when they're sad or in pain. When somebody dies, I become very gentle and kind. I notice the good and kind things people say about those who have died.

As an adult, I seem to be kinder when someone dies. If only I could learn to see the good things about them while they were alive. If only I would tell those around me how much I love them, while I still have the opportunity to do so.

Help me look for the good in those around me, especially those I love the most. Help me live this day as if it were the last. Help me become a more gentle and loving person through my greater appreciation for those around me.

O Mary, Mother most sorrowful, the sword of grief pierced thy soul when thou didst see Jesus lying lifeless on thy bosom; obtain for me hatred of sin because sin slew thy Son and wounded thine own heart, and grace to live a Christian life and save my soul.

Our Father.... Hail Mary.... Glory be to the Father....

Jesus Christ Crucified.
Have mercy on Us.
May the souls of the faithful departed, through the mercy of God,
Rest in peace.
Amen.

13th Station: The body of Jesus is taken down from the cross

Your Thoughts • Your Prayers • Your Dreans

Fourteenth Station: Jesus is laid in the tomb

We adore you, O Christ, and we praise you.
Because by your holy cross You have redeemed the world.

Jesus, your body is prepared for burial. Joseph gave you his own tomb. He laid your body there and rolled a large stone in front of it, then went home. What a sad day it has been for so many people.

As a child, sometimes I try to keep everything for myself. I find it hard to share my things with my brothers or sisters and with my friends.

As an adult, I can be selfish too. I can accumulate things and keep them for myself. I try to make sure I have what I want before I share what I have with anybody else.

Help me think of Joseph of Arimathea, who risked his own life as he accepted Jesus' body for burial. Help me think of how Joseph loved Jesus so much that he gave him his own tomb.

My Jesus, beside Thy body in the tomb I, too, would lie dead; but if I live, let it be for Thee, so as one day to enjoy with Thee in heaven the fruits of Thy passion and Thy bitter death.

Our Father.... Hail Mary.... Glory be to the Father....

Jesus Christ Crucified.
have mercy on Us.
May the souls of the faithful departed, through the mercy of God,
Rest in peace.
Amen.

14th Station: Jesus is laid in the tomb

Stained
Glass
Windows

Your Thoughts • Your Prayers • Your Dreans

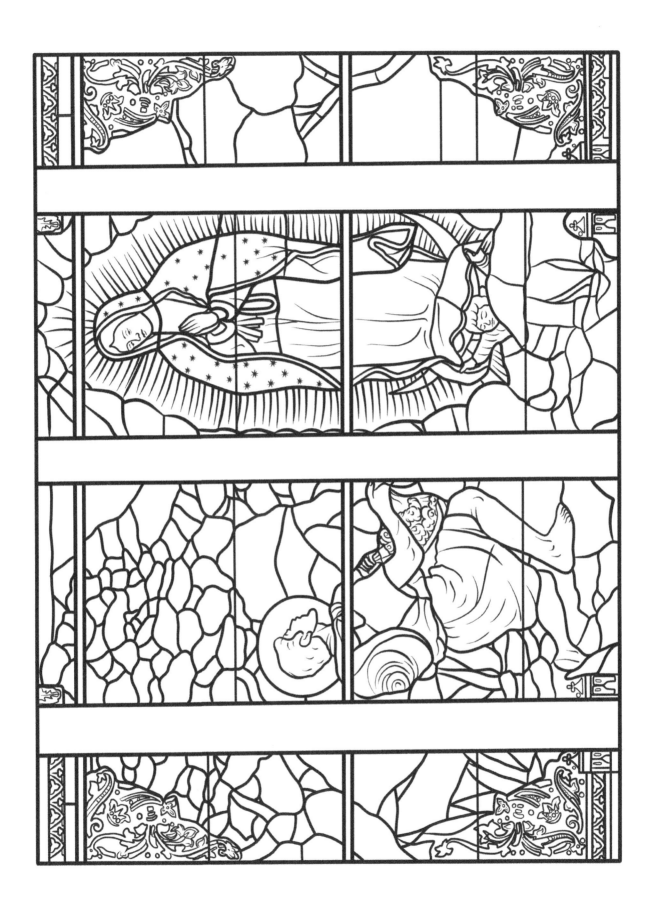

Made in the USA
Las Vegas, NV
23 March 2024

87666643R00046